101 Pep-Up Games for Children

> It is energy—the central element of which is will—that produces the miracle that is enthusiasm in all ages. Everywhere it is what is called force of character and the sustaining power of all great action.
>
> — SAMUEL SMILES

D1221820

SmartFun Books from Hunter House

101 Music Games for Children by Jerry Storms
101 More Music Games for Children by Jerry Storms
101 Dance Games for Children by Paul Rooyackers
101 More Dance Games for Children by Paul Rooyackers
101 Drama Games for Children by Paul Rooyackers
101 More Drama Games for Children by Paul Rooyackers
101 Movement Games for Children by Huberta Wiertsema
101 Language Games for Children by Paul Rooyackers
101 Improv Games for Children and Adults by Bob Bedore
Yoga Games for Children by Danielle Bersma and Marjoke Visscher
The Yoga Adventure for Children by Helen Purperhart
101 Life Skills Games for Children by Bernie Badegruber
101 Family Vacation Games by Shando Varda
101 More Life Skills Games for Children by Bernie Badegruber
101 Cool Pool Games for Children by Kim Rodomista
404 Deskside Activities for Energetic Kids by Barbara Davis, MS, MFA
101 Relaxation Games for Children by Allison Bartl
101 Quick-Thinking Games + Riddles for Children by Allison Bartl
101 Pep-Up Games for Children by Allison Bartl
The Yoga Zoo Adventure by Helen Purperhart

Ordering

Trade bookstores in the U.S. and Canada please contact:

Publishers Group West
1700 Fourth St., Berkeley CA 94710
Phone: (800) 788-3123   Fax: (510) 528-3444

Hunter House books are available at bulk discounts for textbook course adoptions;
to qualifying community, health-care, and government organizations;
and for special promotions and fund-raising. For details please contact:

Special Sales Department
Hunter House Inc., PO Box 2914, Alameda CA 94501-0914
Phone: (510) 865-5282   Fax: (510) 865-4295
E-mail: ordering@hunterhouse.com

Individuals can order our books from most bookstores,
by calling **(800) 266-5592**, or from our website at
www.hunterhouse.com

101
Pep-Up Games
for Children

Refreshing, Recharging, Refocusing

Allison Bartl

Illustrations by Klaus Puth

A Hunter House SmartFun Book

Library of Congress Cataloging-in-Publication Data

Bartl, Almuth.
[Muntermacher-Spiele für Grundschulkinder. English]
101 pep-up games for children : refreshing, recharging, refocusing / Allison Bartl.
p. cm. — (SmartFun activity books)
Translation of: Muntermacher-Spiele für Grundschulkinder.
ISBN-13: 978-0-89793-495-4 (pbk.)
ISBN-10: 0-89793-495-4 (pbk.)
ISBN-13: 978-0-89793-496-1 (spiral bound)
ISBN-10: 0-89793-496-2 (spiral bound)
1. Games. 2. School children—Recreation. I. Title. II. Title: One hundred one pep-up
games for children. III. Title: One hundred and one pep-up games for children.
GV1203.B36 2007
790.1'922—dc22   2007025187

Project Credits

Cover Design: Jil Weil & Stefanie Gold
Illustrations: Klaus Puth
Book Production: John McKercher
Translator: Emily Banwell
Copy Editor: Kelley Blewster
Proofreader: Herman Leung
Acquisitions Editor: Jeanne Brondino
Editor: Alexandra Mummery
Publisher: Kiran S. Rana

Senior Marketing Associate: Reina Santana
Publicity Assistant: Alexi Ueltzen
Rights Coordinator: Candace Groskreutz
Order Fulfillment: Washul Lakdhon
Customer Service Manager:
Christina Sverdrup
Administrator: Theresa Nelson
Computer Support: Peter Eichelberger

Printed and Bound by Bang Printing, Brainerd, Minnesota

Manufactured in the United States of America

9 8 7 6 5 4 3 2 1   First Edition   08 09 10 11 12

Contents

*A detailed list of the games indicating appropriate group sizes
begins on the next page.*

List of Games

Page	Game	Whole group	Any size group	Small groups	Pairs

Preface

Okay, dear teachers and group leaders, the sky is overcast and the children are starting to rub their eyes and yawn. Twenty-eight pairs of bored and tired, but expectant, eyes are directed at you. If you want to keep the children from wandering off on their individual mental journeys, it's time to flip through this book. Pick out a couple of lightning flashes and magically change the room's prevalent gray back into sunshine.

In this book you will find all kinds of energizing ideas—fun activity games, for example, to jump-start circulation. Pent-up energy is the most common cause of irritability, listlessness, aggression, regression, and general bad moods in children.

Using no materials at all, or with everyday objects from the junk drawer, the children can happily dive into these games, helped along by their natural curiosity, excitement, and creativity. Variety is important for them, and these games engage all the senses and ranges of motion in various social combinations.

If the teacher or group leader takes active part every so often it has a positive effect not just on him, but also on the overall atmosphere. Playing together bonds the group, strengthens the "us" feeling, and enlivens tired children. A renewed sense of energy and improved general atmosphere will make it easier for children to follow and concentrate on their lessons for a longer period of time. They will be encouraged to take an active part in school/camp/group life, which will improve both their productivity and their social interactions. In the long run, they will have more fun in these types of situations.

Each of the games included in this book takes only a few minutes and can be used anytime—in class or during breaks or other free time.

There's no room here for curmudgeons and cranks; it's time to play, laugh, and get moving.

For easy reading we have alternated use of the male and female pronouns. Of course, every "he" also includes "she," and vice versa.

Introduction

In this book you will find lively games and practical tips that you can use with elementary-age children anytime as pick-me-ups to counter tiredness or bad moods.

The level of the games' difficulty gradually increases over the course of the book. With a few exceptions, the games at the beginning are easy enough for first-graders, while the ones at the end are more appropriate for nine- or ten-year-olds. However, almost all the games can easily be modified for different ages. The games are listed in alphabetical order at the end of the book.

Helpful Ways to Change the Pace

The best way to prevent tiredness and to keep energy reserves filled is to have plenty of variety in your lessons. Here are some pointers:

- When preparing your lesson, remember to use as many different group-size formations as possible: whole group, small groups, pairs, and individuals.
- Switch off teaching and learning materials, even if it takes time. At the end of the day, it will be worth it if the children are still paying attention.
- Use different seating arrangements; try to sit in a circle more often, and occasionally move the class outside.
- Invite "guest teachers" to come talk to the class (e.g., parents, grand-parents, police officers, the mayor, or any other specialists whose expertise may be useful).
- Create surprises and moments of amazement for the children.
- Never overstuff the children, but instead make them hungry for new knowledge.

Key to the Icons Used in the Games

To help you find activities suitable for a particular situation, each one is coded with symbols or icons that tell you some things about it at a glance:

- The size of the group needed
- If props are required
- If music is required

- If a large space is needed
- If physical contact is or might be involved
- If the activity involves going outdoors

These are explained in more detail below.

The size of the group needed. Most of the games can be played by the whole group, but a few require pairs or small groups, and some can be done individually. All games are marked with one of the following icons:

 = The whole group plays together

 = The children play individually, so any size group can play

 = The children play in small groups of three or more

 = The children play in pairs

If props are required. Many of the games require no special props. In some cases, though, items such as paper and pens, blindfolds, or other materials are integral to running or playing a game. Games requiring props are flagged with the icon below, and the necessary materials are listed under the Props heading.

 = Props needed

If a large space is needed. A large space is required for a few of the games (for example, when the whole group is required to form a circle or to walk around the room). These are marked with the following icon:

 = May require a larger space

If music is required. Only a few games in this book require recorded music. They are flagged with the icon below, and any indications on the type of music are listed under the Music heading.

 = Music required

If physical contact is or might be involved. Although a certain amount of body contact might be acceptable in certain environments, the following icon has been inserted at the top of any exercises that might involve anywhere from a small amount of contact to minor collisions. You can figure out in advance if the game is suitable for your participants and/or environment.

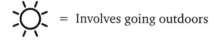 = Physical contact likely

If the activity involves going outdoors. A few games require going outdoors. These are marked with the following icon:

= Involves going outdoors

All Right!

How to Play: Listless, tired, sad, low on energy? Not for long, because now we're going to play All Right! The leader picks one child to call out some instructions; for example, "Let's stand on our chairs!" In response, the others immediately cry out, "All right!" and follow the suggestion. After that it might be, "Let's throw our pencil cases up in the air," or, "Let's shake our neighbors' hands." Each time, all the children yell, "All right!" before following the instructions. After the third time, the person shouting out the instructions chooses a new child to call out instructions by saying, "Now Mariah is going to tell us what to do," and again, the children delightedly cry out, "All right!"

whole group

Backward Theater

How to Play: For this funny theater performance, one "actor" sits on the "stage" (a table, for example) and pretends to be a depressed person. The actor spends three minutes looking silently and seriously at the audience. Meanwhile, the audience members do everything they can to get the actor to laugh, or at least to smile, without touching the actor (so, no tickling). They make faces, tell jokes, and clown around.

Can they get the actor to grin before the three minutes are up? If he grins or the time runs out, the actor chooses a replacement to play in the next round.

Wind-Up Mice

How to Play: The adult leader uses a magic word to change the children into wind-up mice. At the leader's signal, the squeaking mice flit to and fro through the room, gradually moving more and more slowly. As their wind-up mechanisms grind to a halt, they barely make it back to their seats, let themselves fall into their chairs, and come to a complete standstill. Some mice may even run out of power before they get to their desks. These mice are frozen in the middle of the room, and the leader has to give their cranks one more turn to help them reach their seats. As a variation, the children can be divided into two groups that take turns being mice, since watching is fun, too!

Counting Fingers

How to Play: This simple game is a hit with younger children. The leader starts clumsily, but very seriously and industriously, counting a child's fingers. One of the fingers could always have gone missing, you know. Unfortunately, the count reveals only nine fingers. Dismay shows on the leader's face, and he immediately does a recount. Now there are eleven! Oh no, what's going on? He counts again and again, while the child is thoroughly entertained, until finally arriving at the right number. Thank goodness!

5

Fresh-Air Shower

How to Play: The children stand at the wide-open windows and stretch out their muscles; they breathe deeply, audibly taking in the cool, fresh air. After three minutes in the fresh-air shower, everyone sits back down, refreshed and full of energy. The leader can ask children to share with the group how the fresh-air shower made them feel.

Pick-Me-Up Tip: Light is an important energy source, and it's good for fighting low spirits. Let light into the room by opening the curtains and blinds as far as possible and by removing large objects from the windowsill that rob the room of light. In addition, you may be able to replace the existing light bulbs with brighter ones, and also add extra light sources. Sometimes just dusting off the existing light bulbs or lamps helps bring in more light.

Dance School

Music: Suitable for dancing

How to Play: The children all stand next to their chairs and start dancing to some cool music. Suddenly the adult leader calls out a name, and that child gets to be the dance instructor. As the new instructor grooves, gyrates, and gets down to the music, all the students turn to face her and imitate what she's doing. But before they know it, the leader is calling out the next name, and all the students start to copy the new instructor's way of interpreting the music—swinging their hips, maybe, or reaching their arms into the air. At least five dance instructors get a chance to lead the group before the song ends and it's time to sit down.

Thumbless

How to Play: Who can be the first to put on a jacket, take off their shoes, tie their shoelaces, or stick a book into a backpack without using any thumbs? Whoever thinks this sounds easy should get right to work! It's best if children work in pairs. One tries to perform the task chosen by the leader, and the other watches to make sure there's no cheating.

Johnny: "Teacher, would you punish me for something I didn't do?"

Teacher: "Of course not, Johnny."

Johnny: "Good, because I didn't do my homework."

Wind Power

How to Play: Are the children tired and listless? Maybe they need extra wind power! Following the leader's example, everyone stands up, stretching one arm up and the other down. Then the leader and the children all blow and blow until their arms start to move—like a windmill at first (arms move in a circle), then like a big bird (imitate wings flapping). Once they really get going, the leader can have the children move their arms like a helicopter propeller (hold the arms overhead and circle the forearms around each other). Try each of these three moves a few times.

9

 whole group

Song Circle

Prop: A ball

How to Play: Everyone sits in a circle. One child has the ball and starts singing a familiar song. Suddenly, he throws the ball to another player and immediately stops singing. Each catcher takes up the song wherever the last child stopped. If they don't know the words, they have to say so and then start singing a new song. When the song is over, whoever is holding the ball gets to start a new song. The faster the ball is thrown, the more fun the game is.

Variation: To make this game more competitive, change the rules so that if a child is thrown the ball and doesn't know the next words, they are out and have to leave the circle. The game is then played repeatedly until only one player—the winner—remains. To make sure no obscure songs are intentionally chosen to get people out easily, consider making a list of allowable songs from which the children can choose.

The Seat of Transformation

Props: Chairs for everyone

How to Play: The children arrange their chairs in a circle, with one chair in the middle. As the music plays, they run around the outside of the circle. When the music stops, everyone looks for a seat. The seat in the middle is a special one—the child who manages to sit there gets to transform her companions, who have to act accordingly. They could be changed into babies, apes, trees whose branches move gently in the wind, horrifying monsters, or pillars of salt. Then the music starts up again, the spell is broken, and the children run around the outside of the circle again.

whole group

The Nonsense Game

How to Play: The adult leader thinks up a nonsense combination of words; for example, "A bicycle tire filled with lukewarm chocolate pudding." Then he asks the whole group questions that must be answered with this phrase, while they keep straight faces.

Question: What do you want for Christmas?

Answer: A bicycle tire filled with lukewarm chocolate pudding.

Question: What did you have for breakfast?

Answer: A bicycle tire filled with lukewarm chocolate pudding.

Question: What do you put in your backpack every morning?

Answer: A bicycle tire filled with lukewarm chocolate pudding.

The questions and answers continue until one of the children gives in and breaks out laughing. Either the game can end here, or else that child is out and the game continues until there is a winner, the one who keeps a straight face the longest.

Waves of Silliness

How to Play: All the children stand in a circle. The leader chooses one to start a wave of silliness; for example, by wiggling her whole body. Her left-hand neighbor imitates her, as does the next person, and so on until the wiggly wave comes back to the person who started it. Now it's the child on her right's turn to come up with some kind of silly motion. The faster the wave moves, the funnier the whole thing gets. The game continues until everyone is laughing, energized, and ready for the next activity.

Pick-Me-Up Tip: Have especially lethargic children wash their hands thoroughly in cold water.

13

Auntie Bertha's Stroll

How to Play: The adult leader begins by saying: "Auntie Bertha is walking through the park."

In unison, the children ask: "*How* is she walking through the park?"

The leader responds, "Auntie Bertha always walks like this," and demonstrates how Auntie Bertha shuffles, or hops, or waddles, or skips. The children all imitate the walk.

But the leader has already spotted another relative, and calls out, "Uncle Herbert is walking though the park," and the game starts over. Once the children understand how the game works, they can take turns leading it.

Tip: This game is also good for vocabulary practice. Try using several different movement words, like "amble," "shuffle," "saunter," "stride," etc., or different adverbs, like "cautiously," "stealthily," "anxiously," "sullenly," etc.

Red and Black

Props: A deck of cards for each group

How to Play: This competitive game fires up ambitions; the children discover new strengths and release some energy. Afterward, everyone is refreshed and ready to get back to learning.

Divide the players into small groups and have each group decide on an order they will follow in the game. Each group plays by itself. A standard deck of cards is spread out on each group's table, face down. The children take turns uncovering one card at a time. If the card the child turns over is a red card, the child keeps it; if it's black, she turns it back over. This game is played very quickly, and children try to keep track of which black cards have already been flipped over. Whoever ends up with the most red cards is the winner.

 any size

Dancing Feet

Music: Rhythmic

How to Play: The children sit up straight in their chairs and put their shoe-less feet in a row on the floor (rearrange chairs if necessary, or have the children turn sideways in their chairs so their feet are all in a row in the aisle). In time with the music, they lift their heels as far as possible while keeping their toes on the ground. They do this eight times, and then it's the toes' turn. They point up as high as they can go while the heels stay on the ground. The leader gives the instructions for each action. This foot dance works best when done in time with the music. Afterward, the feet are gently shaken out.

Pick-Me-Up Tip: Put a few drops of peppermint oil into a scent lamp with a little bit of hot water. Light a tea candle underneath and be amazed at the positive effect it has on tired children.

Quick Trip to Kalamazoo

How to Play: The children all stand next to their seats. The leader loudly calls out, "One-way ticket to Kalamazoo, and step on it!" Right away the children start running in place. They go faster and faster until they hear the next command: "And now back!" at which point they all turn around and run "back" (while in place) as fast as they can.

Whew! Pretty hard work, but it's gotten the circulation going. Naturally, a child can give the commands instead of the leader.

Tip: In warm weather children can lie on their backs in the grass, pedal their legs in the air, and take a bike ride to Kalamazoo.

Herd of Elephants

How to Play: As long as your room is on the ground floor, you can briefly transform the children into a herd of elephants—and yourself, too! As the leader, you determine the speed at which the herd travels. At first, the herd is far away, and a faint rumble can be heard. Then it comes closer. The stamping of elephant feet grows louder and louder, and the herd seems to be moving faster and faster. Now it's very close, and in addition to the stamping you can hear the elephants loudly trumpeting. But finally the herd has passed; the trumpeting stops and the stomping grows quieter and quieter until there's no noise at all.

Rhinos

How to Play: Out on the playground, the leader can easily transform grumpy or tired children into a herd of rhinos. The children all lean forward, sling one hand across their backs, and hold their noses with the other.

The rhinos stomp around the yard as hard as they can—around trees and bushes, between the fence and the doorstep—and after a few minutes they come back to their starting point. They can only come back when they have turned back into good boys and girls. An important note for each rhinoceros: You are traveling alone and are not allowed to touch your herd-mates. You can make noises if you want, but don't let go of your nose!

Silly Time

How to Play: Laughter is a ready source of energy. Some occasional silliness makes an ordinary day cheerful and keeps the children in good humor. The suggestions below are for things you can do, but you can also use some of them as games the children can play.

Examples

- Call the children "Mr." and "Ms." Younger children particularly enjoy this.
- When speaking, replace all your vowels with "o."
- Mix up the "latters of the elphabet" when speaking.
- Walk through the room like a robot.
- Give the children "silly cookies." Silly cookies are regular butter cookies with funny faces drawn on them in icing (available in tubes at the supermarket).
- Tell a funny story from your life.
- If you know how to juggle, demonstrate.
- Have a child tell a joke, or tell one yourself (you can find several scattered throughout this book).

Indoor Snowball Fight

Props: A lot of old newspapers

How to Play: In the absence of snow, children can ball up pieces of old newspaper. Once each child has a supply of at least ten balls, the fight begins. After three minutes, the fight is over; the children collect the balls and put them in the recycling bin.

Pick-Me-Up Tip: A smile is enchanting and enlivening, and it can create a good atmosphere. Be conscious of this, and try to smile more often. You will be surprised by how quickly your smile is returned to you. Try signing your next homework corrections with a smiley face instead of your initials.

any size

I Like Me!

How to Play: The adult leader says, "It's a good thing we have such long arms! We will now wrap our arms around ourselves and squeeze tight, giving ourselves a big hug. Then we vigorously shake out our arms and shout out *one* thing we like about ourselves."

Variation: The children can do it again and shout out something they like about the person on their left and right, or anyone else they name.

Pick-Me-Up Tip: Bananas are an excellent source of energy and children usually like eating them. If you hand out bananas as rewards for various achievements, the fruit will be even more popular.

- With the skin still on, cut bananas in half lengthwise. Each child then gently scoops out the fruit with a spoon.
- Frozen bananas, cut into slices, provide energy and are refreshing. The children can suck on the icy disks as though they were candy.

any
size

Eeny, Meeny, Miny, Moe

How to Play: The children stand at their places. As soon as the game begins, the children rub their stomachs with one hand and pat their heads with the other. At the same time, they all repeat the phrase, "Eeny, meeny, miny, moe, my shoe is pressing on my toe." Whoever laughs or loses track of the rhythm is out and has to sit down. The game continues until only one player, the winner, remains.

any
size

Peanut Hunt

Props: A large number of peanuts with the shells intact

Preparation: Before the children arrive, the leader hides a large number of peanuts on top of the cabinets, behind the curtains, in the sink, and wherever else that's hidden but safe to get to.

How to Play: As soon as the children start to show the first signs of tiredness, they are challenged to a peanut treasure hunt. They all swarm through the room and look for the little bundles of nutrition. However, children should wait until as many nuts as possible have been collected, then wait for the leader's permission to shell and eat them (so as to minimize the mess).

Tip: Set aside an extra handful of nuts for children who don't manage to find any.

Note: Many schools have policies against bringing peanuts in if they have a student with a known peanut allergy. You may want to check with your school or organization about this ahead of time.

The Serious Laughing Game

How to Play: The children stand at their places. The leader loudly says, "Ha!" and points at one of the children. Deadly serious, the child answers, "Ha, ha!" and points at a second child of their choosing. Also remaining serious, this child says, "Ha, ha, ha!" and points to the next child, who says "Ha!" four times while keeping serious, and so on. Whoever laughs or says "Ha!" too many or too few times is out and must sit down. The next child in line starts over with one "Ha!" Whoever is left standing at the end has won.

Polar Bear Chase

How to Play: For this game, the leader chooses one child to be a polar bear and another to be an Eskimo who's being chased. All the other children form groups of four to five players, and in each of these groups, all but one player, who is chosen by the leader, forms an igloo by joining hands. The last player in each group becomes an Eskimo, who stands inside the igloo. (Any extra children can divide up among the groups, making larger igloos.)

The polar bear chases the free Eskimo around the igloos and tries to catch her. If the chase gets too risky for the Eskimo, the child can hide in the nearest igloo and be safe from the wild polar bear. If she does this, the Eskimo who was living in that igloo has to leave the safety of the igloo and try to avoid being caught by the polar bear. If the Eskimo is caught, the Eskimo turns into the polar bear for the next round of the game and also gets to choose a new Eskimo.

any
size

Fast Forward

How to Play: When the adult leader calls out, "Fast forward," the children immediately transform into energy-filled kids. They run through the room like Charlie Chaplin and clean up their things as fast as they can. If they talk at all, they talk super-fast; they laugh faster, read faster, and do everything they're supposed to do at a very high speed. The epidemic is over only when the leader (who has, of course, also been infected with fast-forward fever) gives the sign; everyone then calms back down and slowly takes a seat.

See-Saw

How to Play: The children pair up. They stand back to back and link elbows. Then they take turns bending forward, which allows them to pick the other child up from behind.

Pick-Me-Up Tip: Tired, sad, lethargic, and listless? Chin up! Hold your back straight and your chest out, and take deep breaths into your belly. Even if it sounds like what your parents always told you to do, it's the quickest pick-me-up I know. Pay attention to the children's posture! Many times, just lifting up their heads helps them feel better because it makes them feel stronger and more self-confident.

Dancing on Paper

Music: Lively

How to Play: Things that initially seem strange to adults are often fun for younger children right away. To start, the children stand at their places and move their upper bodies, especially their arms, shoulders, and heads, freely to the music. Then each takes a pen and transfers the movements onto a piece of paper lying on the table. This should not be a drawing! The lines and circles should look more like traces left behind by ice skaters. After a couple of minutes, everyone stops drawing.

If they wish, the children can take the drawings home and color in all the different areas they have created. This makes some interesting mosaic pictures that would surely be worth hanging up in your room.

Neighbors

Prop: A ball

How to Play: The children make a circle. One child stands in the circle, holding a ball. Suddenly he calls out the name of one of the other players and throws the ball high into the air. The person whose name is called calmly remains where she is, but the two people to either side of her react immediately and try to catch the ball. Whoever succeeds gets to stay in the middle and call out the next name. If no one catches the ball in time, the same player goes again. The faster the game is played, the more exciting it is.

Musical Confusion

How to Play: One child, designated as the guesser, is sent out of the room. The rest of the children think up a three-syllable word, for example, "kangaroo." Then the children are divided into three groups. As soon as the guesser comes back into the room, the leader gives the sign and all the children start singing to the tune of "I'm a Little Teapot," but instead of singing the actual lyrics to the song, they replace each beat with one of the syllables from the chosen word, in the same rhythm and to the tune of the song. The children in group one sing only the first syllable of the chosen word, in this case, "Kan, kan, kan, kan, kan, kan," etc. Group two sings only "ga" over and over, and group three sings only "roo."

In practice, this is just as chaotic as it sounds on paper, but it's a lot of fun. The guesser can stop the "singing" at any time by raising his hand and guessing the three-syllable word. If he's right, he can choose the next guesser. If not, the children keep singing.

Chain Reaction

How to Play: The children form small groups, and each group stands in a circle, facing the center. The leader then points to one child in each group, who then begins the game by making a random motion; for example, turning her head from left to right. The player on her right repeats the first motion and then adds a new one; for example, snapping his fingers. The player on his right, player number three, turns her head, then snaps her fingers, then wiggles her elbows, in order.

The game continues until a player finally forgets one of the motions or mixes up the order in which they occur. That player drops out of the game, and the others continue until one winner emerges. The winners of each group then come together for a final match, or the children can be regrouped so each gets another chance to become a winner.

Pick-Me-Up Tip: Sunlight is the ideal source of energy. If the opportunity presents itself, take the children out in the sunshine for a couple of minutes.

32

The Sick Ballet Troupe

Music: Classical, suitable for dancing

How to Play: Except for one member, the whole ballet troupe has gotten sick. But a performance is scheduled, and there's no way it can be cancelled. So ten children, chosen by the leader, are named to be replacement dancers. They immediately take the "stage" in front of the other children. As soon as the music starts, the "healthy" ballet dancer begins dancing, and the new dancers must all imitate his movements. Of course, this needs to be done quickly, and the movements should be as coordinated as possible so the audience won't notice the substitution.

After a couple of minutes the first group sits down and becomes the audience, and the leader chooses a new healthy dancer and a new group of replacement troupe members to have a turn. This game is fun for dancers and audience members alike!

Paper Race

Props: A sheet of paper for each child

How to Play: All the children stand next to each other at the starting line on the playground. Each child receives a sheet of paper, which she should hold against her stomach or chest, and waits for the starting signal. Then they all take off; by the third step, at the latest, they should all lift their arms above their heads. The "airstream" will cause the sheets of paper to stick to their bodies. The first person to cross the finish line without losing the piece of paper is the winner.

Note: If a player loses the sheet of paper by running too slowly, he must go back to the beginning and start over.

34

Coin Collection

Props: Five coins

How to Play: The leader walks through the room and hands out five coins, one each to any five children. The recipients immediately hide the coins somewhere on their bodies—in a pocket, fist, or any other hiding place that presents itself. Then all the children stand up and wander around the room, singing a well-known song of the leader's choosing. One child is assigned to collect all the coins but must do so in the order in which they were handed out. The object of the game is to remember who has the coins, to approach those children in the order in which the coins were handed out, and to guess where the coins might be hidden.

The collector has to be speedy—the collection time is over as soon as the song ends. This game challenges concentration and memory, and makes the child who manages to complete the task feel very successful.

Variation: To make this game more competitive, each collector can be timed by the leader. If a collector asks a person without a coin, asks someone out of order, or guesses the wrong hiding place, they are out and it's someone else's turn. The player who gets everything right the fastest, wins.

The Giggle Box

Prop: A cardboard box, perhaps covered on the outside with the Sunday comics page

How to Play: Every classroom should have a giggle box. From the outside, it looks like an ordinary cardboard box, but the contents are truly unusual. The box contains funny newspaper articles, jokes, riddles, funny pictures, etc. Each child contributes something. Whenever a child is in need of cheering up, she gets to rummage through the box and pick something out. The item can either be enjoyed alone or shared with the rest of the group. If she chooses to, she can tell the group why this item makes her feel better.

36

Mirror Image

How to Play: The leader picks about ten children to stand in a row; they are the mirrors. The leader then chooses another child to walk from mirror to mirror, making a funny face in front of each one. The mirror imitates the grimace and "freezes" it as soon as the child moves on to the next mirror. This both looks funny and requires a lot of concentration. An observer—either the leader or someone chosen by them—decides which "mirror child" did the best job; that person gets to be the next one to clown in front of the mirrors.

Ball Tag

Prop: A soft ball

How to Play: One child receives a soft ball, such as a Nerf ball, and a second child is chosen to be "It." All the children go for a stroll around the room. Tables and chairs provide obstacles that make the game even more exciting.

The child with the ball calls out another child's name—for example, Reilly—and throws him the ball. As long as Reilly is in possession of the ball, the person who's "It" tries to get to him to tag him. However, Reilly can call out another child's name and toss the ball away to her before being tagged by "It." If "It" succeeds in catching Reilly before he tosses the ball away, they switch roles. Or if the ball fails to be caught by the child whose name Reilly has called, then Reilly becomes "It." This isn't as easy as it sounds; the person who's "It" may have to chase several different children before she catches one with the ball.

small
groups

Kid Sandwich

How to Play: The children are divided into groups of three. One member of each group is selected by the leader to be the "support." This child stands up straight, and the other two lean on him. They can lean with their backs or with their outstretched arms or with one bent arm. The middle child says, "Look out!" and carefully pulls himself out of the middle of the sandwich. The other two should stay as still as possible and keep their balance. It looks like they are leaning on an invisible object. This is good for the muscles as well as for physical control and concentration. Team members take turns being the support and being the leaners.

Once More
with Feeling

How to Play: First, the children decide on a song that everyone knows: "Twinkle, Twinkle, Little Star," for example, or "Jingle Bells." One singer is picked by the leader to choose a particular mood; for instance, irritated, sad, tired, angry, excited, or happy. The children sing the song together with plenty of emotion; exaggeration is of course encouraged.

Pick-Me-Up Tip: Eat small but more frequent snacks to maintain a consistent energy level throughout the day. Tyrone, a good and hardworking student, literally suffered from power failure after every mid-morning recess; he battled tiredness and didn't get his energy back until late morning. This changed when the teacher asked Tyrone's mother to split up his sizeable snack into smaller portions. From then on, Tyrone snacked in three stages and was much more energetic throughout the day.

Seat Protectors

How to Play: The children begin by sitting upright in their chairs. Next, they lean against their seat backs and hold the edges of the chair with both hands. As soon as the leader gives the sign, the children straighten their arms, lift their behinds out of the seats, and pull their knees up as far as possible. Balancing only on their hands, and with their backs still leaning against the backs of their chairs, the children hover over their seats. Gradually, the "seat protectors" run out of steam, and soon they are all sitting back down in their chairs. Whoever hovers the longest wins.

Knock knock.
Who's there?
Little old lady.
Little old lady who?
I didn't know you could yodel!

whole
group

Hand Sandwich

How to Play: Many children will know this game already, but it's even more fun with a big group (divide very large groups into groups of ten or so). One person puts her hand on the table, and another puts his on top of it. In this way, they continue building the tower until all the children have their hands in the sandwich. Ready? The person whose hand is on the bottom carefully pulls it out and places her hand on top of the pile. Then the next person's hand is pulled out and placed on top, and so on. This goes faster and faster until you have a mixed-up mess, and the sandwich is declared "eaten up."

New Seating Arrangement

Props: A box containing slips of numbered paper, prepared in advance

Preparation: On a seating chart, number the seats in random order. Then write the numbers on small slips of paper, fold them up, and store them in a box.

How to Play: When the day's first wave of lethargy hits, the children all pack up their things and come to the front of the room. One at a time, in an order decided on and called out by the leader, they each pull a number from the box and announce it to the leader. Using the seating chart, they find their new seats. Each child sits down and waits to see who his new neighbor will be. There isn't a trace of sleepiness now!

any
size

Mouth Harps

How to Play: One child picks a song that everyone knows. First, they all sing it together. Then each child makes a pout by sticking out their bottom lip and plucks the rhythm of the song on the bottom lip while humming the song. This both looks and sounds funny.

Pick-Me-Up Tip: If you're tired, you may need more sleep. This age-old truism was recently backed up by a study of adolescent children. The more sleep the children got, the fewer behavior problems they exhibited. Thus, "I don't wanna" is often an attitude resulting from too little sleep. This is a topic to discuss not only with the children, but also at the next parents' night. Incidentally, the advice to "sleep yourself into shape" goes for adults, too.

Think Good Thoughts

How to Play: When you think about a nice thing or a friendly person, you feel better right away! Children's attention can be directed toward the positive by giving them specific "good-thought" assignments, for example:

- On your way to school, look for three things you like.
- Try to get three people to laugh or smile today.
- Plan to have three positive experiences next month. What could they be?

- This month is the beginning of winter (or spring, or summer). Name three neat things that happen this time of year.

When children start to show signs of lagging, have them tell the class what funny or cool thing they saw on the way to school that morning—funny graffiti on the freeway underpass, for example, or a foal in the meadow, a dog in a raincoat, etc.

The leader can also ask children to create good-thought assignments for each other or put them in a box and let each child pick one.

"Lisa, do you want to go to the park?"
"I can't. If I leave my dad alone with the computer, he'll start playing again instead of doing my homework!"

Good Posture

Props: A textbook for each child

How to Play: Straight posture is good for the lungs, and as a result it improves oxygen content in the bloodstream. Here's how to make posture training fun: All the children sit up straight in their chairs; each places a textbook on his head and tries to balance it. Now they continue whatever they were doing. If a child loses her book, she quietly sets it aside. The winner is the one who balances the book the longest.

any size

Upstairs, Downstairs

How to Play: The children line up at the bottom of a flight of stairs. They take three steps up, then two steps back down; then they take three more steps up, and two back down, and so on until all of the children have made it to the top.

Variation: Super math geniuses can calculate how many total steps they took, both going up and going down, without counting during the stair climbing. Who can guess the correct answer the most quickly?

47

any
size

Foot Circles

How to Play: All the children sit up straight in their seats and stretch their legs out in front of them as far as they can go. They lift their heels off the floor and point their toes toward the ceiling. Everyone rotates first the left foot, then the right, making ten circles with each. Next they try to move the left foot clockwise and the right one counterclockwise, both at the same time. This requires an enormous amount of concentration. Afterward, have them shake out their feet and enjoy the energy boost to their feet and legs. If they would like, children can share with the rest of the group how the experience felt to them.

any
size

Today Is My Favorite Day

How to Play: Write on the board: Today is my favorite day because...
Each child quietly thinks up one or more reasons why this might be true. Then, following an order decided on by the leader, they take turns giving their best reasons.

Examples

- **Today is my favorite day because** I'm going to the movies with my parents tonight.

- **Today is my favorite day because** my mom is getting out of the hospital.
- **Today is my favorite day because** I got an A in math for the first time.

Of course, the leader gets to complete the phrase, too.

Pick-Me-Up Tip: The color orange counteracts tiredness, depression, and listlessness. If you're hanging up posters with rules or slogans, try writing on orange tagboard. Orange curtains can be invigorating, and a mostly orange picture can be a visual rest stop; children and adults alike can let their eyes wander to it over the course of the day.

"Wash your hands before you go to school," Katie's mother reminds her.

"I don't have to," says Katie. "I never raise them anyway."

Silly Clapping

How to Play: The children play in pairs; team members turn to face one another. They hold their hands at chest level, palms facing their partners.

One child leads the game for the whole class, calling out, "Right!" Immediately, the partners clap their right hands together. Then the game leader calls out "Left!" or "Both!" and the children clap along accordingly. But now the game leader speeds up. She calls out instructions faster and faster, until finally general confusion and laughter reign, and the leader gives up her role to another player.

whole group

Alphabet Circles

How to Play: The children spread out on the playground. The leader draws a circle around each child to make a standing place. Now the adult leader calls out a letter at random; for example, "A." All the children whose first names contain the letter A—as in Martin, Lisa, Aaron, or Frank—must quickly find new circles. Only one person is allowed in each circle at a time.

As this is happening, the leader tries to find a circle for himself, so that one person will be left standing outside. The child who is left over (or the adult leader, if he doesn't succeed in finding a spot) calls out the next letter.

The faster this is played, the more fun it is.

Guided Treasure Hunt

Props: Two blindfolds; a treasure item, such as a bag of gummy bears

Within seconds, this simple game can transform a roomful of tired children into a bubbling cauldron of activity.

How to Play: The children are divided into two groups, and each group chooses one child to be the treasure seeker. The two seekers are blindfolded before they are led to the starting point—the chalkboard, for example.

Once the room is completely quiet, the leader silently puts the treasure (a bag of gummy bears, for example) somewhere in the classroom. Then the game begins: The group members guide their seeker to the treasure by calling out directions—but indirectly, without giving the seeker of the other team any hints. This sounds much easier than it actually is.

Whoever finds the treasure first is the winner, and will obviously be generous and share it with the rest of the group.

52

Lion Hunt

How to Play: The leader starts by saying: "I'm going on a lion hunt. Are you coming with me?"

The children all stand up and shout, "Yes!"

L: "First we have to walk across the meadow." The leader walks in place, and the children imitate her.

L: "Then we get to a lake, and we have to swim." She makes swimming motions, as do the children.

She starts from the beginning, a little bit faster this time.

L: "I'm going on a lion hunt. Are you coming with me?" The children shout, "Yes!"

L: "First we have to walk across the meadow." They walk in place.

L: "Then we get to a lake, and we have to swim." The children all make swimming motions.

Now the story continues:

L: "We have to hack our way through the bushes!" She waves her imaginary machete, and the children imitate her.

L: "Now we're at the foot of a mountain. We're going to climb up!" The leader and the children all make climbing motions.

The leader starts over from the beginning one more time, even faster, and repeats everything up to this point.

L: "There's a dark cave. We have to go inside!" She bends over to crawl into the hole. Suddenly she screams, "Help, a lion!" Instantly, they retrace the entire route in reverse. They scramble down the mountain, fight their way through the bushes, swim across the lake, run across the meadow, and finally make it back home safe and sound!

Tom comes into the room loaded down with sandwiches and drinks. His teacher says, "That does it! This isn't a restaurant!"

Tom says, "I know, that's why I brought my own food."

pairs

Thumb Wrestling

How to Play: Feel like a little wrestling? This competition allows all the children to play at once, and they don't even have to stand up.

First, they pair up and take each other's hands, as illustrated. As soon as the referee gives the signal to start, each player tries to capture and hold down his opponent's thumb. The match is over after just ten seconds. Did any of the wrestlers manage to conquer their partners' thumbs?

Forward, Backward, Forward Again

How to Play: Do the children have to get from the classroom to the yard, or from the art studio back to the classroom? Nothing could be simpler! But they don't just run any which way; that would be much too boring, and it's usually against the rules anyway. In this race, the children take two steps forward, then turn around and take two steps backward (i.e., moving in the same direction they started in and progressing toward the destination). Then they turn around again and take two steps forward, and so forth. Ready? Everyone line up and let's go!

Secret Code

How to Play: Children love secret signals, which connect the members of a group and differentiate them from other groups. Sometimes these secret codes come out of funny situations and are only funny to someone who was there and experienced them. For example, one teacher wanted a student sitting next to the light switch to turn on the light. She misspoke, and for whatever reason said, "Click!" The child didn't understand and looked confused, but the other students shouted in unison, "Light on!" Now, whenever the teacher says, "Click!" in any situation, the children jump up and shout, "Light on!" This inside joke strengthens the group dynamic and always gets the children to laugh. Any children who miss the cue and don't respond are responsible for deciding on the group's next secret signal.

Pay attention if something similar happens in your group, and use it to create your own secret code.

whole
group

One-Legged Tag

How to Play: As soon as the leader starts the game, the children all hop around the room on one leg, trying to catch the other players. A tap on the shoulder from any other player means the child who was tapped is out and has to go back to his seat. The game ends when only three one-legged hoppers are left in the room.

All the players who are out watch to make sure none of the active players sets a second foot on the floor. If someone gets caught doing that, she is out, too.

57

(Don't) Follow the Leader

How to Play: This game is fun because kids get to do the exact opposite of whatever the leader tells them. The adult leader stands in front of the group and calls out, for example, "Day!" In unison, the "followers" call back, "Night!" Then the leader calls out, "Yes!" and the children respond with "No!" and so on.

This goes on for a while until the leader starts adding gestures. He might call out, "Up," and lift his arms up into the air. Immediately, the disobedient followers respond by saying "Down," stretching their arms toward the ground. Then it might be "Sit!" and all the children stand up. Or he might call out "Left," and turn that way, while the followers respond with "Right," and turn in the other direction. Finally, the leader has had enough and cries out, "Everyone stand next to their seats!"—whereupon those awful kids politely sit down in their chairs.

Sit!

Giggly George and Giggly Georgia

How to Play: One child is chosen to be Giggly George (or Georgia). This child's assignment is to get at least three other children to laugh, or at least grin, within a certain amount of time. Naturally, George will choose his victims carefully and approach people who have a little less self-control. George runs to his first candidate and laughs, makes faces, tells his best joke, and clowns around, trying to get her to laugh (but no tickling allowed!).

As soon as that child laughs, George moves on to his second victim. Can he do it? Can his silliness make three children break out in laughter within the set number of minutes?

Pick-Me-Up Tip: The way the day ends is the way children will remember it, and it motivates them for the next day. End your lesson plan a few minutes early so you have time to talk about all the nice, new, and funny things that happened today.

59

Animal Guessing Game

How to Play: This game has two parts: a fairly standard animal guessing game and a practical joke on one of the children.

The leader divides the room into groups. Then she takes one child out of the room and tells him what animal he's supposed to be—a spider spinning her web, for example, or a squirrel jumping from tree to tree. The leader goes back into the room and gives the child a minute to think about his role. Then the actor comes in and acts out the part of the animal. The other children guess. Whoever gets it right earns a point for their group. Then the leader chooses a new actor, and the game continues.

After a few rounds, the leader tells one child to act like a monkey eating a banana. She tells the class, however, that they can guess any animal they like, as long as it's not a monkey eating a banana. The actor thinks he's gotten an easy assignment, but to his astonishment nobody guesses it. He beats his chest and hops around dragging his knuckles in front of the other children, but they guess things like "duck" or "ant" or "elephant" or even "bat." The monkey's actions get more and more exaggerated, and the children are laughing hysterically. Finally, the leader has an idea; a light bulb goes on over her head, and she calls out, much to the actor's relief, "Maybe it's a monkey eating a banana!"

Hula Hoop

Props: Three to five hula hoops are plenty, since most rooms aren't big enough for all the children to play at once.

How to Play: The athletes spread out so they have as much space as possible, and the game starts right away. Experienced children can circle the hula hoop onto one leg, back to their waists, and then onto the other leg. Less-practiced players can at least have the hoop orbit around their arms or necks. Those who have the hip movement down can compete with each other to see who can go the longest.

It's only fair that the adult leader has a turn, too, so with the children's encouragement, the leader can show off his groovy moves with the best of them.

whole group

Night Watchman

Props: A blindfold; a box containing slips of paper prepared in advance, as explained below

Preparation: For each child, write a number on a slip of paper (from one to however many are in the group) along with an animal or an object that makes noise. Fold the pieces of paper and put them in a box.

How to Play: Each child draws a slip of paper and secretly looks at it to see what it says: for example, "18 sheep," "23 tractor," or "5 dog." Then the adult leader designates one child as the night watchman and blindfolds her.

The night watchman calls out a number, and the child who has that number responds with the appropriate sound or animal noise. Using the above examples, if the number five is called, that child starts to bark. If the night watchman identifies the barker and calls out his name, they switch roles. If the watchman doesn't recognize him, she calls out another number.

Variation: If there are several of the same animal in the room, the night watchman might ask all the dogs to bark at once. The watchman should then try to identify at least one of the dogs by name.

Q: What sound do porcupines make when they kiss?

A: Ouch!

whole group

Vowel Race

Props: Chalk, masking tape, or string; five big pieces of paper on which vowels are written, as explained below

Preparation: Mark five areas of the room (draw lines with chalk, masking tape, or string) and designate a vowel for each one. Write each of the vowels on a separate big piece of paper and post the paper in that vowel's area.

How to Play: The leader divides the children into two equal groups and assigns numbers to each player. Each group will have a child who is number one, another child who is number two, etc.

The leader calls out a word containing only one vowel—"skip," for example —and a number, say, "nine." The two children who are nines immediately run to the area with the vowel that corresponds: in this case, "I." Whoever gets there first scores a point for the group. The game continues. "Wolf, number seven!" the leader calls, and two more children race across the room. After about fifteen words, the points are added up, and one group is declared the winner.

63

Speed-Reading Competition

Props: A photocopy of a premade worksheet for each group, as explained below; two pens or pencils per group

Preparation: Write about twenty words all over an 8½ × 11 sheet of paper, vertically, horizontally, and diagonally. Make enough copies for each group of three children to have a copy.

How to Play: The leader divides the children into groups of three. She picks one child to be the judge, and has the other two face off in a speed-reading competition against each other. The leader gives each group one copy of the word sheet.

The two opponents sit next to each other and look at the page. Each holds a pen or pencil to point at the words. Then the judge names any of the words that are on the page. The players quickly look for the word, and the one who finds it first gets a point. Words can be repeated as often as the judge wants. The game is over when one player is ahead of the other by three points. That child then becomes the next judge.

If you want, you can have the winners of each round continue to challenge each other until the competition has one overall winner.

Rhyming Proverbs

How to Play: If the children know what a proverb is, they can play this game. The leader gives the first line of a brand-new proverb, and the children find an appropriate ending for it. If it rhymes, even better!

Examples

If the summer's hot and wet...I'll feel sorry for my pet.

If the summer's dry and hot...I will like the pool a lot.

If a storm should come to pass...the bugs will shiver in the grass.

Variation: To make this game more competitive, the leader distributes a list of five "beginnings" to each child. Each child then has three minutes to come up with the funniest proverb ending that is still appropriate. The child judged by the leader to have the funniest ending for each proverb wins a small prize.

Pick-Me-Up Tip: Flowers are always nice to look at. Choose some bright ones that bloom reliably and as often as possible. Avoid cacti. A "tree" in the corner of the room can be decorated differently throughout the year. Sometimes it can be hung with handmade birds, sometimes with colorful paper hearts. Easter eggs hanging from colorful ribbons turn it into a spring tree, and at Christmastime it can contribute to the room's décor when decorated with strands of lights and homemade stars.

Q: What is small, green, and triangular?
A: A small, green triangle.

65

Word Ball

Prop: A ball

How to Play: The children stand at their seats. As the ball is thrown from child to child, following an order previously made clear to the children by the leader, each catcher has to name a word. The words all belong to a category; they could be related by topic, part of speech, or ending. Whoever drops the ball or can't think of a word within a few seconds must sit down. The last child standing is the winner.

any size

Careful Listening

How to Play: At the beginning of the day, write three different words on the board. Tell the children that you will be using these words several times over the course of the day. As soon as you say one of the three words, the first child to notice it calls out, "Stop!" and gets a point for paying attention. Whoever has the most points at the end of the day wins.

Q: How do you stop a charging elephant?

A: Take away its credit cards.

Knife, Fork, Scissors, Light

Preparation: Practice the commands.

"Knife": The children all hold their arms straight at their sides.

"Fork": The children stretch their arms upward on either side of their heads.

"Scissors": They swing alternating arms up and down.

"Light": The children switch their hands "on" and "off" like a light, first making a fist and then spreading out their fingers.

For all four commands, the children must stand up.

How to Play: The leader gives the first command: "Hocus pocus, all the children turn into knives!" They all jump up and stand like knives. The last one to follow orders, and anyone who acts out the wrong thing, is out and stands to the side.

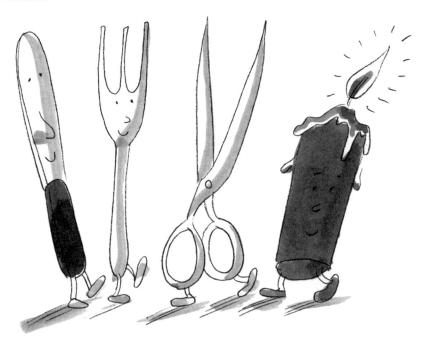

The rest of the children sit down again and listen for the next command. The game is played until about three-quarters of the group is out. The rest of the children can celebrate their victory.

The game is more exciting the faster you play.

Variation: If the leader leaves off "hocus pocus" at the beginning of the command, that means the command should not be followed, and the children stay seated. Anyone who stands up is then out.

whole group

68

Partner Search

Props: A box; premade paper slips, as explained below

Preparation: On each of two slips of paper, write the title of a well-known song, like "I'm a Little Teapot"—in other words, two slips will say "I'm a Little Teapot," two might say "Jingle Bells," and two might say "Twinkle, Twinkle, Little Star." Make enough for each child to draw one slip. The papers are folded and placed in a box.

How to Play: Each child draws a slip of paper and starts singing their song when the signal is given to start. The players are all singing simultaneously, so they must listen carefully to each other's singing since each now has to find the other person who is singing the same tune. Pairs that have found each other quickly compare slips of paper just to make sure, and then quietly stand with the leader and enjoy the rest of the chaotic singing.

Multiball

Props: Four balls of different types

How to Play: This is a game to pep up even the most maxed-out kids! The leader chooses eight of the sleepiest-looking kids to stand in a circle. One child, picked by the leader, gets a ball and throws it to any other player; this player catches it and immediately passes it on to someone else. The ball is thrown from child to child, making sure that each player gets the ball only once, until it comes back to the first player, at which point round two starts. *Note:* The route taken by the ball in the first round must be exactly the same for the subsequent rounds. Each player has to remember who threw her the ball and to whom she passed it.

Now the leader throws a second ball into the circle. This one is passed along following the same route as the first. Then a third ball is added, and maybe even a fourth, which requires even more concentration and coordination. It's even more fun if the balls are different; for instance, if you play with a handball, a ping-pong ball, a medicine ball, and a balloon.

Once the first eight players have perked up, each gets to choose a new player to replace them in the next round of the game.

Variation: To make this game more competitive, change the rules so that if a player makes a mistake they are out and have to choose a new player to take their place and start the next round.

Lucky Sixes

Props: Two dice for each group; pens or pencils; paper

How to Play: The leader divides the children into several groups, and each group sits at a table. The leader then picks one child from each group to start, and following a clockwise direction, the players quickly take turns going around the circle and rolling one die until a six comes up. The player who rolled the six immediately grabs the second die and starts rolling it as many times in a row as possible. The points are added up; the player rolling the second die should say each revised total out loud so the others can check her math. While this is going on, however, the rest of the players take turns quickly rolling the first die; as soon as someone else rolls a six, the first child's playing time ends. Her total is written down, and it's now the next player's turn. The winner is the person who has the most points at the end.

Body Instruments

How to Play: First, the children think of noises they can make with their bodies (besides talking, singing, or humming): clapping, finger snapping, stamping, knocking, or whistling. Then they all sing a song together, and each musician accompanies the song with a different "instrument."

After that, the same melody is played using only the body instruments.

Variation: You can also make this a guessing game. One child is sent out of the room while the others decide on a song. Then the guesser comes back in, and the rest of the children perform the "instrumental" version of the song. Can the guesser figure out what the song is?

Pick-Me-Up Tip: Success makes a person happy, brave, and self-confident. With your camera, capture as many of the children's successes as you can, and hang the pictures up in the room. Make sure each child has at least one personal achievement that qualifies them for the "Wall of Fame."

72

Math Gymnastics

How to Play: The children stand at their places. Choose a multiplication table for them to recite in unison forward and backward—for example, sevens or threes. As they recite the multiplication table, they do a knee bend or a jumping jack for each calculation.

Pick-Me-Up Tip: Everyone has a chance to win an Oscar! Make a statuette out of paper cups covered in gold foil, and glue a plastic figurine on top, spray-painted gold. (Brand-name plastic figurines can be found cheap at garage sales.) Anyone who does something remarkable—carrying a sick friend's backpack home, improving her spelling-test score by a significant number—earns the Oscar, which is ceremoniously awarded at the end of the day. If someone receives the award three times (keep careful track), he gets to keep it forever. Alternatively, tape two paper cups together with the openings facing each other, and put a small prize inside. The Oscar winner gets to keep the prize but gives the statuette back.

whole group

A, E, I, O, U

Prop: A soft ball

How to Play: The children stand at their seats for this short, energizing game. The leader tosses a small, soft ball to one of the children and says, "A." The catcher then throws the ball to someone else and says, "E." The ball is then tossed back and forth across the room one time for each of the remaining vowels (i.e., "I," "O," and "U"). The child who ends up with "U" throws the ball at anyone she wants, trying to get them out. If she succeeds, the child who was hit is out and has to sit down, but first gets to start the ball moving again with "A." If the last child catches the ball instead of being hit, the thrower is out.

The game continues until approximately half of the children have taken their seats.

Pick-Me-Up Tip: Anticipation can be a powerful energizer. If your children know that a fun game or a video is coming up, they'll get through the day with a lot more pep.

Classroom Ping-Pong

Props: Two ping-pong balls; a book for each child

How to Play: The children play against each other in two groups. Half of each group stands against one wall, and the other half stands against the other wall. Each child holds a book, and one child in each group gets a ping-pong ball. At the starting signal, the two players with the balls run to the opposite wall, holding their books in front of them and bouncing the ping-pong balls on the books. If a ball falls to the ground, the child who dropped it has to go back to the wall and start over. As soon as a player makes it to his team on the other side, the first person on that side takes the ball and carries it back the same way, bouncing it on a book. The balls are transported back and forth across the room; the first team to have all its members carry the ball across the room is the winner.

Song Variations

How to Play: One child is sent out of the room to be the guesser. The leader picks a familiar song and tells the children one word in the text that will be replaced by another word. For example, if the song goes, "Froggy went a-courting...," the children might sing, "Doggy went a-courting...." The guesser comes back into the room, and the others start to sing the song. It's even harder if they all sing at different times.

As soon as the guesser has found the mistake, he raises his hand, and the singers immediately stop. If he's right, he gets to choose the next guesser. If his guess is wrong, the song starts up again.

Playing Detective

Props: Candy, cookies, or other items as rewards

How to Play: As soon as they hear a knock at the door, the children need to be perfectly attentive. With great concentration, keeping silent as mice, they pay attention to the guest's every move; they hang on every word and try to remember every detail of the visitor's clothing, hairstyle, etc. Once the guest has left, one child gets to pose three questions; for example, "What were the first four words Mrs. Doodleby said? What color are Mrs. Doodleby's shoes? How many pieces of paper was she holding?"

The first children to answer the questions correctly each get a "Surveillance Sucker," or maybe an "Observational Oatmeal Cookie," as a reward.

Class Clown

Preparation: Make sure the children are familiar with the meaning of the term "class clown," and tell them to prepare for when it's their turn.

How to Play: If there's a general bad mood in the room, one child who volunteers gets to be the class clown. This is a much harder assignment than you might think, because getting a whole group of children to laugh takes self-control and courage. The class clown tells her very best jokes, and tries to tell them cleverly. If they want, children can perform a skit alone or with a friend; they can sing, rap, or show the group funny pictures (from the Internet, for example). The class clown has five minutes to cheer up her compatriots. If after the the time runs out the leader holds a vote and the majority of the children feel cheered up, she gets a small prize or reward.

Note: To encourage positive votes, the leader should remind the children how hard it is to perform for and be judged by others. Sensitive children should probably not be encouraged to play the class clown unless they want to.

any
size

Portable Pick-Me-Ups

How to Play: If you notice that your group is lethargic, use the next break to turn the children themselves into pick-me-ups. Their assignment is to cheer up the other children during the break with nice compliments, small courtesies, and a friendly attitude. After the break, the children have a few minutes to share their experiences—if and how they succeeded in cheering up the others. The nice thing about this? Successfully cheering other people up makes you cheerful, too—happy and strong.

whole
group

Hidden Treasure

Props: Three small objects children can sit on

How to Play: One child is sent out of the room. The leader gives three other children small books (or some other small object, such as a knit cap, a chalkboard eraser, or a thin folder) to sit on.

   The first child is called back into the room and now has to figure out which three children are hiding something. He only has the amount of time it takes the class to recite a multiplication table chosen by the leader backward and forward (or sing a song or recite a poem, etc.).

Variation: To make this game more competitive, the child looking for "treasure" is out if she fails to make the correct guesses in time or if she makes an incorrect guess. Players who guess correctly and in time are given a small reward or treat.

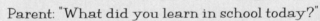

Parent: "What did you learn in school today?"
Student: "Writing."
Parent: "And what did you write?"
Student: "I don't know. We don't learn reading until next week."

whole group

The Black List

Preparation: Make a list of the small but annoying things that bug you and the children about the room. There might be a table leg that always snags socks, an old poster on the wall that everyone is tired of, an ancient cactus that's about to die and pokes everyone who tries to close the curtains, etc. Ask the children what bothers them, too. At least ten things can be put on the "black list."

How to Play: The next time a sleepy fog closes in over your room, take a five-minute break. Let one child pick something from the list, and fix it then and there. Everyone will be glad to cross that annoying item off the list!

Countdown

How to Play: The children take their starting positions as rockets, crouching down next to their seats. In a robotic voice, the leader intones: "Ladies and gentlemen, only twenty seconds remaining until liftoff!" The rockets all start their engines, and the sound of howling motors intensifies. "Nineteen," announces the leader, with a close eye on the second hand of her watch, and then stops counting out loud. When the children think the time is up, they jump up and lift their arms above their heads. More and more rockets take off into the sky. Once the last rocket has been fired, the children all sit back down. Then the leader names the children who really started at exactly twenty seconds. There might even be time for another round.

Quick-Break Exercises

Music: Rhythmic

How to Play: All the children march around the room in a line, in time with the music; they lift their knees up high and swing their arms. When the leader says, "Stop!" they all stand still and follow her command to do a leaning, bending, hopping, or stretching exercise. Then they start marching again, until the next command to stop.

If the leader ever has to leave the room for a moment, a child can be put in charge of this game and give the commands. This keeps the group productively occupied.

any size

Alarm!

Prop: A kitchen timer

Preparation: Set a kitchen timer to go off after about thirty minutes

How to Play: For children who are about ready to drift off into dreamland, this fitness game is just the ticket. As soon as the timer goes off, the children all jump up and run in place—fast at first, then even faster—until the timer stops buzzing and they can all sit back down. For the next few days, even pointing out the set timer will be enough to get their heart rates going.

The teacher welcomes the principal to the classroom and casually asks, "How long are you going to stay with us today?"

Principal: "Till I get on your nerves."

Teacher: "Leaving so soon?"

Memory Lane

Prop: A ball

Preparation: Think of something you have done together as a group.

How to Play: "Do you remember our field trip to the Sacramento River?" the leader asks, and throws a ball to one of the children. The child's job is to mention some detail about the experience, for example, "I remember that Lisa's baseball cap got blown into the river and floated away." Then he throws the ball to another child. She in turn might remember the horses that the children fed or the funny monk who told them jokes in the mission garden.

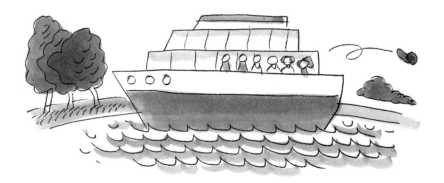

Each child should make a contribution, even if it's only, "I drank three large Pepsis!" At first, the remembering might start out slowly, but gradually the children will remember more and more details and grow more animated.

For the next game, you might reminisce about the first day of school, a summer picnic, or the play you put on for the parents.

Creepy Wilbur

How to Play: One child leaves the room. The leader picks another child to be "Creepy Wilbur" (or Wilma). As soon as the first child comes back into the room, all the children except Creepy Wilbur start calling out "Cream of Wheat, Cream of Wheat," and Creepy Wilbur yells his own name, just as loudly. If the guesser manages to find Creepy Wilbur within thirty seconds, the child whose identity is discovered leaves the room and becomes the next guesser. The first guesser gets to choose the next Creepy Wilbur/Wilma. If the guesser doesn't find her, Creepy Wilma gives herself up and chooses her successor.

Pick-Me-Up Tip: When students are supposed to concentrate on something new, they need, first of all, a free workspace, a clear view, and a receptive attitude. Make sure you take the time to clear off work surfaces between lessons. Items that have nothing to do with the next lesson are distracting and make it harder for children to concentrate.

whole group

Sentence Scramble

Preparation: Come up with a five-word sentence, prefereably a well-known saying, such as "Every rose has its thorns."

How to Play: One child is sent out of the room, while the others split up into five equal groups. The leader calls out any phrase with five words and then assigns one of the words to each group. Each group then calls out their word to the first child as soon as he rejoins the party. The children in group one call out, "Every, every, every...." At the same time, the children in group two call out, "Rose, rose, rose...," and so forth. As soon as the guesser thinks he recognizes the phrase, he raises his hand. The other children immediately fall quiet. If the phrase that the guesser says is correct, he gets to choose the next person to be sent out of the room. If it's incorrect, the children go back to bellowing their words.

whole group

87

Alphabet Chair Grab

Props: Chairs for every child except one

How to Play: The children sit in a circle in their chairs. One child stands in the middle. The children receive pieces of paper, each with a different letter on it. Uncommon letters like X and Q are left out and replaced with Th- and Qu-. Okay, here we go!

The child in the middle of the circle names any word (i.e., "pear"); the only rule is that it cannot have any repeated letters. The children with the letters P, E, A, and R must immediately get up and find new seats. While they do this, the child in the middle tries to grab one of the free seats. Whoever is left without a seat sits in the middle and calls out the next word.

Tip: Clever leaders make sure that sleepier-looking children get more common letters like E, A, I, O, N, S, R, and T, so that they're moving around as often as possible.

 **88**

Mythical Creatures

How to Play: The leader asks questions that can only be answered with "yes" or "no." But instead of saying "yes," the children bark like dogs and beat their wings like geese. If the answer is "no," they croak like frogs and beat their chests like apes. All set? Let's go! "Can crocodiles lay eggs?" asks the leader, and sets off a roar of barking and flapping wings, since the answer is "yes." Did someone let out a croak or forget to flap their wings? That "animal" gets a minus point. Three minus points mean you're out. But the game continues: "Does a leap year have 364 days?" Now the chest-beating frogs take the field—everyone knows that a leap year has 366 days.

The guessing continues until only the three best mythical creatures are left to enjoy their victory.

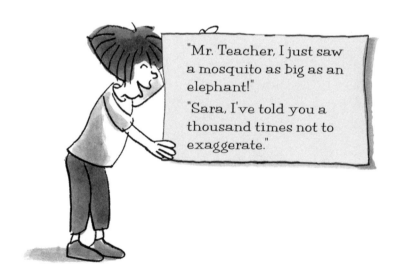

"Mr. Teacher, I just saw a mosquito as big as an elephant!"

"Sara, I've told you a thousand times not to exaggerate."

whole
group

Band-Aid Ball

Props: A ball; several Band-Aids with words written on them, as described below

Preparation: Take several Band-Aids and use a permanent marker write a letter, a whole word, or a number on each; stick the first one to a ball.

How to Play: Two children sit or stand at least fifteen feet apart, but ideally up to thirty feet apart. They roll the Band-Aid ball back and forth. Two guessers run alongside the rolling ball (one on either side of it), trying to figure out what it says. Whoever guesses it first is the winner and takes over for one of the rollers. A new Band-Aid is stuck to the ball, and the next round begins with two new guessers.

Variation: You can also have small groups of children stand to the left and right of the ball as it rolls. Whoever guesses the right answer then scores a point for the group.

Zoology

How to Play: Here's a quick-response game for clever kids: The children rest both hands on the edge of the table. The leader loudly and clearly recites everything they have learned about cats, for example. "Cats are mammals and have two to six young in a litter. Cats are good hunters," etc. When the leader says something silly—for example, that cats spread their wings and fly around catching bats, or that they drink sugar water through their trunks, the listeners yell, "Stop!" and throw their hands in the air. The first one to call out and lift both hands is the winner. She gets to continue the zoology lesson, on any animal she wants—honeybees, sparrows, snakes, etc.

91

any
size

Rhyming Couplets

How to Play: Who can write the best rhyming couplet using the key words they are given?

For the words "loud, teacher, bread," the results could look like this:

The teacher wasn't very loud;
He ate his bread, and then he bowed.

The teacher says these words out loud:
"Who stole my bread? That's not allowed!"

Loud and clear the teacher's voice:
"I'm eating bread, and that's my choice!"

At the end, the winner is determined by a vote. You can set a time limit of a few minutes, or have the winner be the first person to come up with an acceptable rhyme.

Name Bingo

Props: A four-by-four bingo grid sheet; a pen or pencil for each child

How to Play: Each child gets a sheet of paper with a four-by-four bingo grid drawn on it. When the leader tells them to start, the children spend three to five minutes walking around the room and getting sixteen different people to sign their names in the boxes. Each name can be used only once. Children can also put their own name in one of the boxes. Then the children sit back down and hold their boards and a pen at the ready.

In the meantime, the leader has written each child's name on a slip of paper, folded it, and placed it in a box. Now she draws a name and reads it out loud. The children all look for the name on their bingo boards, and cross it out if they have it. The game continues until one player finally has four boxes marked horizontally, vertically, or diagonally and calls out, "Bingo!"

The game keeps going until there are five winners.

The Good Fairy

Props: Three sticky notes

Preparation: Before the children arrive, list activities on three sticky notes and hide them

How to Play: The leader tells the children he has turned into a good fairy and has hidden three little sticky notes in the room; on each one, he has written an activity that will come to pass as soon as someone finds the note. For example, the first note has a die drawn on it, which represents a group game. The good fairy might stick this one to the window behind the curtains. The second one, stuck to Tim's backpack, has a teacup on it that represents a short tea break for everyone to unwind. The third note has a running stick figure that stands for a refreshing jog around the building. This one might have been stuck to the good fairy's back, under a pile of notebooks, on the mirror, in a flowerpot…

The children spend a predetermined amount of time looking for the notes, and if that time expires without the children finding all of them, the activity can continue during any periods of free time that come up during the rest of the day. To encourage the children, each time a child finds one of the notes they are given a small reward or treat.

any
size

Fitness Race

Props: Several items to serve as visible place markers

How to Play: On the playground, lay out several markers about thirty feet apart; use a gym bag, a big rock, a backpack, etc. Have all the children run from the starting line to the first marker, turn around and run back, turn around again and run to the second marker, etc. If you want, you can set up additional rules: doing three knee bends (or jumping jacks, or push-ups) at each marker, running backward to the starting line, or jumping on one foot.

If you set up several courses at once, the children can compete against each other in groups.

any
size

Helicopter Fleet

How to Play: The indoor airfield is super busy today! There's a fleet of helicopters on the runway. The pilots stretch out their arms (propellors) and move them in a circle—slowly at first, then faster and faster, until finally they take off and zoom around the room. Of course, the helicopters make a lot of noise. Fortunately, though, the air-traffic controller soon gives them the signal to land.

The helicopters land in their spots. The flight noise ebbs and disappears completely once all of the aircraft are back in their places.

any size

Whistling Footrace

Props: A piece of chalk or two ropes to create a starting line and a finish line; a whistle

Preparation: Mark lines on the playground

How to Play: Out on the playground, a starting line and a finish line are drawn about fifty yards apart. The racers are at the starting line, with the leader standing about halfway down the track. As soon as the whistle is blown to start, the children run toward the finish line. But when they hear a second whistle, they all turn around and run back. The leader blows the whistle again; they all turn around and run back toward the finish line. The running and the whistle-blowing continue until gradually, guided by the leader, all the runners reach the finish line. As soon as each child crosses the line, they get to catch their breath a safe distance away from the runners who are still running.

Pick-Me-Up Tip: Approximately 75 percent of the human brain consists of water. When the water content in the brain drops below a certain limit, we feel tired and listless. So let the children drink as much water as they want. Incidentally, water peps you up faster than coffee!

97

any
size

I Feel Bright
Yellow Today

How to Play: Yellow, orange, and red are colors that brighten spirits and can improve the mood in a room. In the dead of winter, declare a yellow (or red, or orange) day: "Tomorrow we'll all wear something yellow!" As a surprise, hand out yellow gummy bears or grapes during recess.

Tip: Bring a few extra yellow accessories in case some children don't manage to find anything in their own closets or they have forgotten to wear yellow.

Row Your Boat

How to Play: We know you know this song. Even very young children learn it early and are proud of knowing all the words:

> Row, row, row your boat
> Gently down the stream.
> Merrily, merrily, merrily, merrily,
> Life is but a dream.

The children sit on the floor in pairs, facing each other. They put the soles of their feet together and hold hands. Then they move their upper bodies back and forth in time with the song, leaning way back and then forward. When one child leans back, the other goes forward, and vice versa.

The faster you sing, the faster the motions get. This game wakes up sleepy children in no time and satisfies children's natural need for movement.

whole group

Syllable Shuffle

Props: Chairs for everyone plus one more

How to Play: The children and the leader all sit with their chairs in a circle and leave one chair empty. The leader sits to the left of the empty chair and announces that they are now all in the zoo, and are looking for animals with extra-long names. The leader then starts the game by saying, for example, "I see a crocodile." The other children repeat the word in unison, emphasizing the syllables. Then the leader loudly says, "cro," and slides into the empty chair. The child next to her says, "co," and sits in the leader's vacated chair. The next child to the left says, "dile," and also scoots over one chair. The person now sitting to the left of the empty chair gets to name the next animal. It might be an *o-rang-u-tan* or a *drom-e-dar-y,* an *em-per-or pen-guin* or a *sal-a-man-der.*

small groups

100

Anticipation Calendar

Props: Poster board and art supplies to create several large calendars

How to Play: There's always something to look forward to: the next vacation, an excursion, a trip to the local children's theater, or a school festival. Have the class break up into four or five groups to create anticipation calendars, one for each of several upcoming events. A calendar helps build the anticipation, and looking at it helps brighten many a gray minute in a boring day. During an art lesson, the groups can make posters saying, for example, "Five more days until Christmas vacation," and decorate it appropriately. Each day, a different child gets to pin up a piece of paper on each calendar showing how many days are left.

Only ⑤ more
days until
Christmas vacation!

101

Calculation Ball

Prop: A ball

Imagine a fun way for children to do mathematics. The children stand at their seats. As the ball is thrown randomly from child to child, each catcher has to choose a number, name a calculation method, or provide the answer to the equation. For example, the first child to catch the ball calls "four," the second child yells "times," and the third child calls "eight." The fourth child would then have to reply "thirty-two" when she catches the ball. Whoever drops the ball or can't think of a number, calculation method, or the correct answer within a few seconds must sit down.

The equations should be kept simple and limited to four children at a time. The leader can also limit the range of numbers and calculation methods to make sure they are not too challenging for the group. The game becomes more exciting the quicker the ball is passed around!

Teacher: "Wow, Karl, that was great! Only four mistakes! Okay, let's try the second word."

Alphabetical List of Games

Games with Special Requirements

Games Requiring Props

Games in Which Physical Contact Might Be Involved

Games Requiring a Large Space

Games Requiring Going Outdoors

Games Requiring Musical Accompaniment

SmartFun activity books encourage imagination, social interaction, and self-expression in children. Games are organized by the skills they develop, and simple icons indicate appropriate age levels, times of play, and group size. Most games are noncompetitive and require no special training. The series is widely used in schools, homes, and summer camps.

101 RELAXATION GAMES FOR CHILDREN: Finding a Little Peace and Quiet In Between by Allison Bartl

The perfect antidote for unfocused and fidgety young children, these games help to maintain or restore order, refocus children's attention, and break up classroom routine. Most games are short and can be used as refreshers or treats. They lower noise levels in the classroom and help to make learning fun. **Ages 6 and up.**

>> 128 pages ... 96 illus. ... Paperback $14.95 ... Spiral bound $19.95

101 PEP-UP GAMES FOR CHILDREN: Refreshing, Recharging, Refocusing by Allison Bartl

Children get re-energized with these games! Designed for groups of mixed-age kids, the games require little or no preparation or props, with easier games toward the beginning and more advanced ones toward the end. All games are designed to help children release pent-up energy by getting them moving. **Ages 6–10.**

>> 128 pages ... 86 illus. ... Paperback $14.95 ... Spiral bound $19.95

101 QUICK-THINKING GAMES + RIDDLES FOR CHILDREN

by Allison Bartl

The 101 games and 65 riddles in this book will engage and delight students and bring fun into the classroom. All the games, puzzles, and riddles work with numbers and words, logic and reasoning, concentration and memory. Children use their thinking and math and verbal skills while they sing, clap, race, and read aloud. Certain games also allow kids to share their knowledge of songs, fairytales, and famous people. **Ages 6–10.**

>> 144 pages ... 95 illus. ... Paperback $14.95 ... Spiral bound $19.95

101 LANGUAGE GAMES FOR CHILDREN: Fun and Learning with Words, Stories and Poems

by Paul Rooyackers

Language is perhaps the most important human skill, and play can make language more creative and memorable. The games in this book have been tested in classrooms around the world. They range from letter games to word play, story-writing, and poetry games, including Hidden Word and Haiku Arguments. **Ages 4 and up.**

>> 144 pages ... 27 illus. ... Paperback $14.95 ... Spiral bound $19.95

101 MUSIC GAMES FOR CHILDREN: Fun and Learning with Rhythm and Song by Jerry Storms

All you need to play these games are music CDs and simple instruments, many of which kids can make from common household items. Many games are good for large group settings, such as birthday parties, others are easily adapted to classroom needs. No musical knowledge is required. **Ages 4 and up.**

>> 160 pages ... 30 illus. ... Paperback $14.95 ... Spiral bound $19.95

101 DANCE GAMES FOR CHILDREN: Fun and Creativity with Movement by Paul Rooyackers

These games encourage children to interact and express how they feel in creative ways, without words. They include meeting and greeting games, cooperation games, story dances, party dances, "musical puzzles," dances with props, and more. No dance training or athletic skills are required. **Ages 4 and up.**

>> 160 pages ... 36 illus. ... Paperback $14.95 ... Spiral bound $19.95

101 DRAMA GAMES FOR CHILDREN: Fun and Learning with Acting and Make-Believe by Paul Rooyackers

Drama games are a fun, dynamic form of play that help children explore their imagination and creativity. These noncompetitive games include introduction games, sensory games, pantomime games, story games, sound games, games with masks, games with costumes, and more. The "play-ful" ideas help to develop self-esteem, improvisation, communication, and trust. **Ages 4 and up.**

>> 160 pages ... 30 illus. ... Paperback $14.95 ... Spiral bound $19.95

101 IMPROV GAMES FOR CHILDREN ... by Bob Bedore

Improv comedy has become very popular, and this book offers the next step in drama and play: a guide to creating something out of nothing, reaching people using talents you didn't know you possessed. Contains exercises for teaching improv to children, advanced improv techniques, and tips for thinking on your feet — all from an acknowledged master of improv. **Ages 5 and up.**

>> 192 pages ... 65 b/w photos ... Paperback $14.95 ... Spiral bound $19.95

THE YOGA ADVENTURE FOR CHILDREN: Playing, Dancing, Moving, Breathing, Relaxing by Helen Purperhart

Offers an opportunity for the whole family to laugh, play, and have fun together. This book for children 4–12 years old explains yoga stretches and postures as well as the philosophy behind yoga. The exercises are good for a child's mental and physical development, and also improve concentration and self-esteem. **Ages 4–12.**

>> 144 pages ... 75 illus. ... Paperback $14.95 ... Spiral bound $19.95